The
Integrity
Advantage

The
Integrity
Advantage

Adrian Gostick and
Dana Telford

Foreword by Mitt Romney

Gibbs Smith, Publisher
Salt Lake City

First Edition
07 06 05 04 03   5 4 3

Text © 2003 by Adrian Gostick and Dana Telford

Published by Gibbs Smith, Publisher
        P.O. Box 667, Layton, Utah 84041
        Orders: (1-800) 748-5439
        www.gibbs-smith.com

Book design by Gotham Design, NYC

Printed and bound in the U.S.A.

Library of Congress Cataloging-in-Publication Data

Gostick, Adrian Robert
The integrity advantage / Adrian Gostick and Dana Telford; foreword by Mitt Romney—1st ed.
    p. cm.
ISBN 1-58685-246-9
1. Business ethics. 2. Integrity. 3. Success in business. 4. Competition.
I. Telford, Dana. II. Romney, Mitt. III. Title.
HF5387.G673 2003
174'.4—dc21

To our wives,
Jennifer and Melinda,
whose integrity inspires us.

MELALEUCA HIGHLIGHTS and INDEX

Covered in the August issue of *Leadership in Action* and now a National Bestseller, ***The Integrity Advantage*** poignantly addresses the competitive advantage of integrity through the mouths of some of America's most successful CEOs, including Melaleuca's Frank VanderSloot! Quoted numerous times, Frank's life lessons on integrity and his principles-based approach to business shine through in this excellent best-selling book. Some highlights include:

Page 39 - "Says Frank VanderSloot (Melaleuca), "For people to be totally honest, I think we have too be able to laugh at ourselves and not take ourselves to seriously. If we demand from ourselves perfection, if we never allow ourselves to be imperfect, we are more likely to be dishonest in an effort to protect ourselves from being deemed imperfect."

Page 69 – As a boy, Frank VanderSloot (Melaleuca) doesn't remember his father ever saying a word about integrity. "But I never saw him tell a lie. And I never saw him exaggerate. That had a big impact on me. But I've also been around people who really touted themselves as being honest and ethical. And, without exception, they were trying to convince themselves as much as someone else that they were honest."

Contents

Acknowledgements

This book began with an idea from Christopher Robbins at Gibbs Smith, Publisher. We had commented that during our work with organizations throughout the world, businesspeople who had been successful over the long-term almost always displayed impeccable integrity. To us, it indicated that personal integrity is a competitive advantage in business. And yet, we noted, the subject of integrity seemed to be little more than a passing thought at business school.

Christopher noted that there were a few ethics textbooks in the market, but no work had been published that discussed integrity in action, integrity from a real business leader's perspective. He is the reason this book has been written, and we thank him for his vision and guidance during its creation.

We began this process by talking with Joe Badaracco of the Harvard Business School, most likely the world's premier thinker on ethics and the author of the best-selling book *Defining Moments*. Joe was intrigued by our premise of interviewing business leaders about real-world integrity and suggested the following: "Have them conjure up in their minds two pictures: someone they have worked with who does have integrity and someone who does not. How do they distinguish between the two?" The valuable time Joe spent with us was the genesis of our research and we thank him for his work on this subject and his generous sharing with us.

Next, we express our appreciation to Don Graham of the *Washington Post*, who was our first CEO interview, and the many other visionary leaders we spoke with— from Sao Paulo, Brazil, to Toronto, Canada; and from Washington, D.C., to Houston, Texas. They donated valuable time to this work; indeed, they are at the heart of it. And we are pleased that, to a person, they felt *The Integrity Advantage* was a worthwhile cause. We thank them wholeheartedly.

We wish to thank our contributor, Christie Giles; our editor, Madge Baird; our publicist, Alison Einerson; and our designer, Richard Sheinaus.

We also wish to express a heartfelt thanks to those who helped to organize our interviews for this book: Pam Gazenski, Eleanor Mascheroni, Catherine Collora, Kerstin Sachl, Kate Baum, Catherine Goetschel, Tom Conway, Conn Jackson, Rosely Zambaldi, Wendy Bannahan, Tara O'Donnell, Jennifer Sexton, Josh Tolman, Kimberly Moore, Marsha Merritt, Sharon Tarver, and Tagg Romney.

And finally, we wish to thank our families and our work associates, who encouraged the research and the compilation of what they believe is an important and necessary book.

Foreword

by Mitt Romney
Governor of Massachusetts
Former president and chief executive officer, Salt Lake Organizing
Committee for the 2002 Olympic Winter Games

Integrity is consistency between actions and values. A person of integrity lives in conformity with his or her principal values. "Their word is their bond." An enterprise of integrity likewise does what it says it will do. For a society to thrive, such integrity of word and action is essential. If individuals don't abide by their word, fundamental relationships of trust—such as marriage and family—are in jeopardy. If enterprises don't honor their commitments, substantial commerce is impossible: the essential commercial concept of contract, where one party provides a good in reliance upon a promise that the other will make future compensation, cannot exist if promises are routinely disregarded. It has been observed that the greatness of a society is proportionate to its citizens' propensity to honor a contract.

The heritage of our American nation includes a profound reverence for integrity. In my view, this flows from the character of some of our earliest leaders. In one speech, characteristic of others he would make, Abraham Lincoln took a position that would end up costing him his race for U.S. Senate vs. Stephen Douglas. The country could not survive, he charged, as a house divided, "half-slave and half-free." He knew the likely consequences of his words: "I would rather be defeated with this expression in the speech . . . than to be victorious without it."

The integrity that cost him the senate seat won him the presidency. It probably also inspired the nation to prevail in Civil War and to free the slaves. To some extent, Lincoln's integrity shaped our young nation's values and defined what it means to be American. The measure of a nation is as grand as its past and present leaders.

More lasting than a president's politics and policies is the legacy of his integrity. We are greater as a people, more powerful and successful as a nation, because of Washington, Adams and Lincoln; because of Eisenhower, Truman and Reagan.

I have found that the wages of integrity accrue to individuals as well as to nations. Individuals of integrity enjoy greater success, happiness and even health. Some years ago, a young venture capital firm I had helped found was laboring with seemingly intractable conflicts between our key people. My cofounder had decided to leave, other partners were eyeing the door, and those who, like myself, were committed to staying, were burdened with the constant conflict and criticism. One of my colleagues had heard of a "team-building" company on the West Coast: a few psychologists had developed a one-week program that had reportedly helped dysfunctional teams. It was worth a try.

The extent of our criticism problem became evident in one of our early sessions. The practice was to have each member of the team (we had six in attendance) openly and honestly describe the things he would change in each other and the things he would keep the same. The "target" individual was not permitted to reply or defend. The session was scheduled to last one to two hours, but ours took the entire evening and the next morning: our list of *changes* for others set new records in inventive criticism. It was hard for me to see how we would ever be able to keep together as a firm. It was also hard to see how a beef session was going to help anything. In fact, I believe that the value of the entire program for us was contained in a final, one-hour exercise.

Our instructor claimed that if an individual lives in conflict with his "core values," he will be unhappy, unhealthy and less successful. "Internal conflict between how one lives and what one values creates stress, and stress . . . well, we've all heard about the consequences of stress." Further, if individuals in a group have widely divergent core values, it will be very hard for the group to work together successfully and productively. If he were right, I had my answer as to why our team was disintegrating: our values were miles apart. One partner had said his life ambition was to be in the Forbes 400 list of wealthiest people, another wanted fame and recognition to compensate for his life's early indignities and another cared primarily about his family life. Our instructor acknowledged that what we said we wanted from life seemed quite different, but he said that it was possible that our actual core values weren't that disparate. Perhaps what we were working for, saying to ourselves that we wanted from life, was in conflict with our core values. Well, that begged the question, how do you know what your core values are?

Core values. He instructed us to list the five people we respect most. These could be living or dead. I chose Jesus Christ, Lincoln, Washington, my father, and Joseph Smith, the founder of my faith. Next, we were to write next to each name the three characteristics we most associated with that individual. I chose words like service, love of others, integrity, faith, compassion, vision, strength of character. Finally, we were to select the three words that appeared most frequently on our list. Mine were love, service and faith.

I wondered what my partners' lists would show. With such different life objectives, it would surely be an interesting comparison. It was, but not in the way I had expected. We had all arrived at basically the same values: love and service were unanimously included. The people we most admired all included Lincoln. Others were also common among most of us.

So, we were not so different after all. Our conflicts flowed from the lack of integrity between what we each valued most and how we were conducting our business. I can't say that our business suddenly transformed into an enterprise of love and service, but I can say that it, and we, changed. And we worked together, relatively productively, for another ten years, for which I give a good measure of credit to what we had discovered about ourselves.

Many of the most public failures of our institutions can be traced to the failure of leaders to conduct their enterprise with integrity. In late 1998, it came to light that the men who had led Salt Lake City's bid for the 2002 Olympic Winter Games had provided gifts and payments to the selection committee and the International Olympic Committee well in excess of Olympic rules. One official labeled the conduct "bribery." Congress investigated, Justice indicted, and criminal charges are still pending. IOC members were dismissed. Bad conduct is not unusual. But what was notable was that the people, the community, and the institutions involved would consider themselves to have high ethical standards. Even the word *Olympic* connotes an exemplary level of honor and integrity.

It's not hard to find what went wrong. Winning the bid became too important. And ubiquitous in the justifications by those involved was the phrase "everyone else has done it." Ultimately, and fortunately, I believe that lessons which would have taught that winning is more important than honor and that cheating is acceptable if it is widely practiced, were erased by the response of the community and by the Games themselves. Initially sickened by the bid scandal, Salt Lake wondered if it should cancel the Games. But recognizing that it had made a commitment upon which many now relied, it went forward. And it did so in remarkable ways. Almost $100 million in donations was raised from individuals and institutions, a record. Twenty-three thousand people gave seventeen days as Games volunteers. And, despite extreme cold, the Salt Lake volunteers did not drop out at the 15 percent plus rate expected from the experience of prior Olympics: less than 1 percent gave up! When it was all over, Dick Ebersol, NBC's Olympic head, remarked that the Games had been the most successful ever.

One Olympian at the Salt Lake Games faced her own test of integrity. Vonetta Flowers was offered the chance to join Jean Racine on the number one women's U.S. bobsled. Proven year after year as the fastest sled in the world, Vonetta would become the first African American to win gold in the Winter Games. But to join sled one, Vonetta would desert her long-standing teammate on sled two. Loyalty to her friend would have to give way to winning the gold. Instead, Vonetta's integrity meant that she would place friendship ahead of winning. She stayed on sled two.

The cheers for sled one as it bested the European competitors' times were predictable from the largely American audience. But those for sled two surpassed them when it then beat the entire field. Vonetta's tears that night as she was presented the gold to the strains of the national anthem held greater meaning than usual. She had chosen loyalty and integrity above winning the medal, and for that, she truly deserved it.

Part One

The Truth
About
Integrity

Remember when the good guys always won? The Lone Ranger never failed to catch the bandits, John Wayne's troop took the hill and Wonder Woman's gold lasso couldn't miss?

Some people would have you believe those days are gone. They'll tell you (with a wink) that these days, nice guys finish last.

If that's what you've been hearing, may we respectfully suggest you're running with the wrong crowd. And we've got some folks we'd like you to meet.

They include some of the most respected business leaders from across North America. People like Jim Burke, former CEO of Johnson & Johnson; Shelly Lazarus, chairman and CEO of Ogilvy Mather Worldwide; and Henry M. "Hank" Paulson Jr., chairman and CEO of Goldman Sachs Group, Inc.

They'll tell you—like they told us time and time again during the past year—that integrity is alive and well in the most successful people and long-lasting corporations. In fact, they claim it's darn near impossible for a person to have enduring success in business without a reputation of trustworthiness and integrity.

In the following chapters we'll pass on to you the

incredible wisdom these leaders have taught us during our interviews. We'll share their great advice on what integrity is, why it's important, how a person with integrity acts, and, most importantly, what it takes to become that type of person.

So let's begin. At Harvard Business School in the late 1990s. . . .

• • •

Amidst the pristine pillars and hallowed halls of Harvard Business School, the distinguished business guru Warren Buffett had just delivered a thought-provoking, often irreverent, speech to the newest generation of MBAs. When he opened the floor to questions, the erudite class was not the least bit intimidated, and a dozen raised arms immediately greeted Buffett. He pointed to a student near the front.

"Mr. Buffett," she asked, "How do you make hiring decisions?"

A snicker ran through the audience. "She must be a second-year looking for work," whispered one student to his neighbor. Buffett didn't pause; he had been asked that question many times. He lowered his wrinkled brow and smiled.

"I look for three things," he said. "The first is personal integrity, the second is intelligence, and the third is a high energy level." He paused and ran his fingers through one bushy eyebrow. "But," he said, drawing closer to the microphone and his attentive audience, "If you don't have the first, the second two don't matter."

With the recent scandals at some corporate behemoths, corporate ethics and personal integrity are on everyone's lips these days—in the media, around tables in boardrooms, even across backyard fences in the heartland of America. What they're saying is that employees don't trust their leaders anymore.

It's showing up in surveys across the country, such as the one conducted by Watson Wyatt. The survey confirms that worker trust and confidence in senior management have fallen over the past two years (*Potentials*, September 2002). The survey of 13,000 employees reveals that fewer than two out of five (39 percent) say they trust senior management at U.S. companies. Yikes!

El Paso Corporation is one of the largest energy companies in the country. From his office in Houston, Texas, Executive Vice President and Chief Administration Officer Joel Richards told us, "It's really bad when you introduce yourself as a corporate executive and have to apologize for it. But with the regrettable events of the past year, the general public tends to paint all business executives with the same brush. We have no integrity, no honesty—we are all crooks. That's very unfortunate, because it's just not the case among the majority of business executives. For most of us, integrity is very important."

That's the thing about reputations. They're sensitive things. They can be lost in a moment—and take years to rebuild. Unfortunately, it's a reality some businesspeople don't grasp until too late.

For Matt Cooper (not his real name), the cost of earning up to $150,000 per sale was spending every day lying to his customers. It was the promise of those huge bonus checks that led him to join the sales force of an Internet company in his early twenties. Says Cooper, "If you didn't lie, you were fired. It always came down to careful wording and fudging numbers."

Cooper and his colleagues sold advertising space on the company's Website, promising a certain minimum number of impressions on the client's banner ad and guaranteeing a certain amount of resulting sales. "We could deliver the impressions, but you can't guarantee sales," he adds.

Obviously, contract renewals were zero. He eventually

stopped answering his telephone because the irate phone calls were wearing on him. Next came the death threats.

Finally, Cooper had had enough. He couldn't take the lies anymore. He couldn't look himself in the mirror without wincing. He quit his job, vowed never to lie again, and found a workplace that holds its sales people to much higher ethical standards. He now says that building long-term relationships with trust at the core equates to a better business strategy— not only for your own well-being, but for the well-being and financial health of your company.

Cooper is absolutely right about integrity impacting corporate bottom lines, says Ilene Gochman, Watson Wyatt Practice Leader for Organization Measurement. "There's a strong relationship between trust and employee commitment. When there's no trust, people stop working extra hours and don't put their full effort into their projects."

It's a vicious cycle. Employees don't trust leaders without integrity. They feel no commitment to putting forth their best effort. Production sags, so leaders must find new ways to hide the downturn from shareholders. And the cycle begins again. Fudging can become an ingrained part of a corporate culture.

Find it hard to believe? Here's a scary statistic: Data shows that sometime this week, nearly half of all businesspeople in

North America will lie to a client, to a boss or to an employee. (*Sales & Marketing Management,* July 2002).

Consider the talented manager who worked at one of the much-publicized and much-beleaguered corporate giants during the glory years of the mid-1990s. The man had a graduate degree from a prestigious business school. He foresaw the turbulent waters ahead for his company but was torn, since he stood to gain significant financial reward if he stayed on board for another year.

He remembers the day he realized he needed to leave this company. It was during the required weekly managers' conference call that included leaders on every continent. As an agenda item, one of the executives expressed his concern that managers were not deleting e-mails fast enough. He thought there was too much information out there about the company's activities. This was an agenda item: deleting crucial information because it could potentially be used as evidence.

Luckily, our friend quickly packed his bags, leaving a good deal of money on the table but keeping his integrity intact.

Why didn't alarms go off in other managers' heads? Because their corporate culture had taught them that covering things up was all right. It was all in another day's work.

Diane Peck, former senior vice president of human resources at Safeway, believes it has to do with the culture of the organization. "How people behave tends to be dependent upon the environment in which they operate, the leaders for whom they work. Peer and organizational pressure do a lot to dictate how people behave. So when I read about what happened at Enron, I would bet money that it was a place where people were encouraged, if not required, to push the envelope."

Why were they—and other organizations like them—pushing the envelope? Money. For the record, the pursuit of profit isn't inherently bad. But the pursuit of wealth without the critical counterbalance of integrity can blind individuals—and entire organizations—to the immorality of their actions.

As Millard Fuller, founder and president of Habitat for Humanity International, puts it, "By age twenty-nine, I was a millionaire. My mission statement was 'Get Rich.' This became all-obsessive. You become addicted to it. It is like drugs or alcohol. No matter how much you make, you want more. There's no such thing as enough."

Similarly, when J. D. Rockefeller was asked how much money was enough, he smiled and replied, "Just a little more."

There is a good deal of risk associated with making the

pursuit of short-term personal gain one's highest and most urgent priority. Look at the track record of companies like Enron, WorldCom, Arthur Andersen and others. They made big splashes but were torpedoed by the poor decisions of a few people. As a result, they couldn't stay afloat for the long-term.

Says Jim Burke of Johnson & Johnson, "Trust is absolutely key to long-term success."

But most of all, integrity is important because the very pursuit of it brings out our best selves. "It completes us," says Hank Paulson, chairman and CEO of Goldman Sachs Group, Inc. "To me, integrity, the root word, really has to do with the whole man, with character, with completeness and goodness. I think of a man or woman of integrity as someone who is balanced and complete, with high character. A person of principle."

Are you that type of person? The next part of this book will help you find out.

Part Two

What Integrity Looks Like— Close Up

"Help us to do the hard right against the easy wrong."
—An old church-school prayer

There are some things we do without even thinking. We don't know why. We don't question it. We simply act. Most of the time, those are the things that get us into the most trouble.

When we were young, our mothers used a familiar line whenever we asked to do something that "everyone else" was doing. They would say (repeat along if you know this one by heart), "If all your friends were jumping off a cliff, would you jump, too?"

According to some of North America's most respected business leaders, there are some written and unwritten rules of business that are just plain wrong when you look at them from a perspective of integrity. How many of us are on the proverbial edge of the cliff—with casualties occurring all around us—and we fail to recognize the danger?

In this section, we are going to get to the heart of integrity in action. Not surprisingly, it's hard for people to describe integrity. Definitions are easier. The latest version of Merriam-Webster's dictionary defines integrity, as it applies here, as firm adherence to a code of especially moral or artistic values.

Those we interviewed for this book offered their own definitions.

Jim Burke (Johnson & Johnson) calls it, *"providing a mechanism for individuals and organizations to trust you."*

Millard Fuller (Habitat For Humanity) describes integrity as *"a consistency and steadfastness in your life with what is truthful and what is right."*

Shelly Lazarus (chairman and CEO of Ogilvy Mather Worldwide) says a person with integrity *"puts forth a set of beliefs and then acts on principle."*

Wayne Sales (president and CEO of Canadian Tire) puts it very simply. *"It means doing the right thing."*

Diane Peck (Safeway) believes that *"each individual must define integrity for him or herself."*

There's the rub. We each define the word based on our own knowledge and experience, based on our own view of the world. That only serves to confuse the issue and makes our goal of clarifying the concept more difficult. So, we had to dig deeper. The follow-up questions—the next two, in fact—gave us the truly valuable insight we were looking for. What are synonyms for integrity? Most importantly, how does a person with integrity act?

The list of synonyms for integrity grew with each interview, finally to include honest, trustworthy, truthful, credible, believable, steadfast, good, complete, character, consistent and right. These words make general sense. They are fairly consistent. They are positive words. But how can someone translate these ideas into action? Isn't that what we're grasping for, something far more concrete than words?

Based on our time observing and interviewing influential CEOs, leaders and top executives around the world, we have identified ten characteristics that are consistently displayed by people with a high degree of integrity. Keep in mind that this model represents a sliding scale. Someone who does all ten things all of the time has near-perfect integrity. But that notion is in many ways unrealistic; we each fall short in one way or another.

The Ten Integrity Characteristics are:

1. You know that little things count.
2. You find the white (when others see gray).
3. You mess up, you 'fess up.
4. You create a culture of trust.
5. You keep your word.
6. You care about the greater good.

7. You're honest but modest.

8. You act like you're being watched.

9. You hire integrity.

10. You stay the course.

You may not agree with all of our conclusions, but we invite you to proceed with an open mind. We believe that by integrating these steps into your everyday behavior, you will gain the Integrity Advantage.

Integrity Characteristic #1

YOU KNOW THAT LITTLE THINGS COUNT

There's a story about two frogs placed in a pot of warm water to make soup. The first smelled the onions, recognized the danger, and immediately jumped out. The second frog hesitated—the water felt so good—and decided to stay and relax for just a minute. He rationalized that he would jump out before too long. As the water temperature increased, the frog adapted, hardly noticing the change—until it was too late. Alas, he was made into very delicious frog-leg soup.

That's how businesspeople lose their integrity—a little bit at a time, until they're in a lot of hot water and have nowhere to turn.

The erosion of a person's integrity is rarely quick and spectacular as in a Hollywood blockbuster. It usually occurs as a gradual slipping of standards that is hard to spot—and hard to stop—until it reaches a devastating end.

In the mid-twentieth century, for example, a public company was expected to keep its books in a strict manner. However, those accounting standards gradually eroded until, in 2002, many corporations were caught in the snare of corruption. Warren Buffett, CEO of Berkshire Hathaway, Inc., was one investor who saw it coming. In Berkshire Hathaway's annual reports for the last two decades, Buffett prophetically reminded investors that accounting standards were eroding. He warned them that even respected businesses were fudging to make quarterly numbers. He concluded that fudging would eventually give way to fraud.

Says Don Graham, *Washington Post* CEO, "If you're shuffling orders around, pushing stuff into the pipeline to make one cent more this quarter, it's easy to slip up." That's exactly what happened in 2002.

"Disclosure is an interesting example of what was once a normal standard that has eroded," adds Graham. He points to Benjamin Graham (no relation) of Columbia Business School, who wrote the basic book on the evaluation of securities, *Security Analysis*, in the 1930s. In the 1960s edition, the last in which he participated, Ben Graham wrote: "Prior to the SEC legislation it was by no means unusual to encounter semifraudulent distortions of corporate accounts. The misrepresentation was almost always for the purpose of making the results look better than they were, and it was generally associated with some scheme of stock-market manipulation in which the management was participating. In our 1934 and 1940 editions we gave considerable attention to misleading artifices. But if we repeated the examples here, we should ourselves be misleading, in that we might influence the reader to believe that they are related to present-day practices.... Our considered opinion is that intentionally deceptive reports—which constituted a very real abuse before 1933—are now so infrequent and unimportant as to permit us to dismiss the subject here" (*Security Analysis: Principles and Techniques*, Fourth Edition, Graham, Dodd and Cottle, McGraw-Hill, 1962).

"There you have the dean of securities analysis, a man who spent his working life going over corporate financial statements, saying that as of the early '60s corporate financial statements could be trusted by skeptical people doing careful business analysis. And clearly by the time you get to Enron forty years later, that is no longer true," says Don Graham.

The most shocking thing to him about Enron was that the numbers presented to the public turned out to be completely fictitious. Not surprisingly, investors reacted by pulling their money out of the stock market in record numbers.

"Not only Enron, but WorldCom, too, is an illustration of a company presenting financial statements sworn to by eminent auditors, that were misleading in the most important respects. No investor, however diligent, could have figured out the true financial condition of that company from the published statements. That's a long way from Ben Graham in 1962," says Don Graham.

How did basically good people move so far from accepted standards in such a short time?

"Warren Buffett talks about how most companies were expected to behave in a pretty rigorous way, but then people who cut corners were acclaimed for it. He writes that CEOs, including some very good people, began feeling that if they weren't cutting corners they weren't doing the right thing for their shareholders," says Graham.

The potential end rewards for shareholders grew so big that executives felt justified in taking any means to secure them. For many executives, it was a short leap from there to justifying bigger rewards for themselves.

"The theory behind stock options as a key component of executive rewards was that they would focus the attention of relevant executives on the growth of the company. [The idea was] that as the stock price in the company grew, managers would prosper. But the rewards became very big, and there's some question as to whether the CEO's role ought to be to promote the highest stock price in the short run for the business or to promote the long-term growth of the value of the business. And I don't think those two things are the same," says Graham.

"The right goal seems to me to run the company in a way that builds value for the shareholders over the long-term. To me, that is what shareholder-focused management will do. Another is that the company has the responsibility to communicate the challenging issues it faces as well as the good things. Enron had the stock price in the elevator. The focus was the stock price. That's not the focus in most good companies," Graham adds.

We are talking about very smart, very capable people that went astray, says Joel Richards, chief administration officer at El Paso Corporation.

"At Enron in particular, I am amazed at how the executives could justify to themselves what they were doing. I was talking to one of my colleagues last night, and we said to each other, 'How could you ever justify writing big company checks out to family members of senior executives?' "

Adds Richards, "I think a big part of the problem with some business leaders is arrogance and an overwhelming desire for power and the wealth that comes with it. The whole idea of wealth accumulation somehow got out of whack. Millions and millions of dollars, and all of a sudden, millions aren't that much. It seems that you must be able to convince yourself that what you are doing is somehow okay. You make a questionable decision to make some money. Then you do something else to cover it up, and then something else. The problem gets bigger and you must involve more people, and it just snowballs."

Adds Jorge Paulo Lemann, Brazilian business owner and a member of the board of directors of Gillette, "Many of my colleagues, since they were dealing with the state in some form or another, got into the practice of being corrupt because it was a fast way to get rich. Some of them did reasonably well for a while, but they eventually forgot how to run a business properly. They thought the whole world was dependent upon buying somebody or paying someone off. One by one they gradually disappeared. And the guys who were trying to run their businesses on an ethical basis, they lasted much longer."

Jim Burke (Johnson & Johnson) believes that in these situations, basically good people get tempted to make one small, wrong decision. "You get away with it and then all of a sudden it feeds on itself. Eventually you get caught."

"As a kid, people start out stealing candy bars, not cars," says Frank VanderSloot, president and CEO of Melaleuca, a

$500-million consumer products company. "The fraud you see happening in corporations on a large scale started out on a small scale. People justify wrongdoing in their minds: The company owes me this. But then it grows and fraudulent behavior becomes easier to justify. It can start with a pilfered pen or another simple deception. After a few years, you have an employee who is willing to extort thousands of dollars."

That's why at VanderSloot's company, employees are taught to take the high road on everything, especially the seemingly trivial.

"Little things count," he says. "Like when someone calls in to talk to a manager and [his] assistant says [he is] in a meeting when [he is] not. It's the little things that your employees notice. So we teach employees that we never lie. The assistant may say the manager cannot take the call right now, but we do not make up stories. We will not say anything that is untrue."

Many who fall into the trap of greed and dishonor had unblemished track records before their indiscretions. However, having proved themselves and received more responsibility and autonomy, they find themselves in a situation where no one is looking over their shoulders. The stakes get higher as you climb the ladder. That's when some people falter and start to undertake small deceptions that lead them down a dishonest road.

"There is a Danish saying, 'A bag full of money is stronger than two bags of truth.' Part of what this is saying is that one indication of whether a person has integrity is how they have been tested and how much they have been tested," says Harvard ethics researcher Joe Badaracco.

People who maintain their integrity throughout their careers decide early that they will never break their personal code of conduct. They will remain true to what they believe is right, despite the allure of money, power or popularity. Many of the leaders we talked to used the same phrase: a line in the sand. People with integrity, they say, draw a line in the sand at some point in their careers and are not willing to cross it, no matter the benefit, no matter the threat.

"But truth be told, I don't think there are very many people who have drawn lines in the sand for themselves," adds VanderSloot. "I think the person is rare who has said, 'Regardless of how much it is to my advantage, I'm never going to say something that is not totally accurate.'

"I think most people want to believe that of themselves, but when really put in a bind, they'd be willing, without too much pressure, to say something that was untrue if they felt that was part of their survival mechanism or popularity mechanism or to their benefit somehow," concludes VanderSloot.

But people with integrity are not like most people.

Summary

To have the Integrity Advantage, you do not lie or cheat on the small things; and, as a result, you are not corrupted by the larger temptations—the lure of power, prestige or money. Just as importantly, if you have integrity, you stick to your internal code of morality, even at the risk of losing your comfortable place in the world.

Integrity Characteristic #2

YOU FIND THE WHITE (WHEN OTHERS SEE GRAY)

It was the movie *Spiderman* that started the conversation. As we left the theater, a group of us were talking about how much we enjoyed the show and the special effects. Someone asked, "If you could have any superpower, what would it be?" Someone wanted to fly. There were votes for X-ray vision and superstrength. Then someone stopped the conversation cold by saying, "I'd want to have the ability to know instantly and absolutely right from wrong. To know the truth."

Ah . . . would that it were that easy.

In the work world, we all encounter gray areas. They emerge when we are faced with a right-versus-right decision. Or, simply, when the right thing to do is unclear. And honestly, the farther you rise in an organization, the harder the decisions become and the more tough, gray decisions you face.

Fortunately, you don't have to possess superhuman powers to get to the right decision. What you do need is an unwavering commitment to spend the time and energy necessary to figure it out.

"If there is any question if something is right or wrong, or if this will impact your integrity, you can't just say, 'maybe it's okay.' A person with integrity finds out," says Joel Richards (El Paso Corporation). "People tell me after they are caught, 'I really didn't think it was a problem.' Well, they should have checked it out, and if they had even an inkling that it was inappropriate, they should not have proceeded.

"If you get to the point of having to justify something, you should really talk to somebody, you really ought to think it through and figure out, is it worth it," says Richards.

Often, in the hustle and bustle of business, those inklings (triggered by our instinct or conscience) come at the most inconvenient times. If we listen, they would require us to slow down and reconsider our decision—usually when every minute counts. In a hurry to move forward, we quiet these important warning signals by telling ourselves, "No one will ever know," "I'm just doing what management would want me to do," or "I'll do it differently next time." Usually these and similar phrases are used to justify incorrect choices, to make ourselves feel better about a decision that simply does not sit right.

The next time you find yourself saying those things, that's the precise moment to slow down and take a second look.

Joe Badaracco (Harvard) has written extensively on managing the gray areas in business, and bending the rules versus breaking the rules. He's intrigued by gut-wrenching, sleepless-night decisions we make as businesspeople. He says a lot of business is played in the gray realm.

"There are cases where games are played. You may announce you will build a plant in Saginaw because you want a competitor to think so. But you are really going to build it in Tallahassee. Is that a failure of integrity? I don't think so. Because there is a certain amount of gamesmanship in business."

He sees business, on occasion, as being like a poker game. "There are poker players who have a lot of integrity but still bluff very successfully when they need to. But playing with integrity means you don't have cards up your sleeve."

However, many of the leaders we talked to did not share Badaracco's belief in business gamesmanship.

Frank VanderSloot (Melaleuca) questions how customers and potential business partners would judge the bending of the rules in Badaracco's Saginaw plant example. Would they believe the individuals involved were straight shooters? If, through a merger or other alliance they were to do business with those same competitors at a later date, would the game players be seen as trustworthy?

Adds Shelly Lazarus (Ogilvy), "I don't think that kind of gamesmanship is acceptable. I think there has got to be a way to do business without violating the principles [for] which you stand as a company or as a brand or as an individual. We've got to be competitive, but we've got to think of other ways of being competitive [other than misstating the truth]."

Another controversial theory advanced by Badaracco argues that the mark of a person with integrity is the quality of deliberation in making a tough decision—perhaps as much as the decision itself. He encourages us to move beyond the simplistic right-versus-wrong view of business and realize that we are often faced with decisions that can go either way.

Wayne Sales (Canadian Tire) isn't quite so sure. He says doing the right thing is often clearer than it might first appear.

"Making a decision usually means taking one of two roads. One is doing the right thing. To take the other road, you have to sit back and spin a story around the decision or action you are taking. If you find yourself thinking up an elaborate justification for what you are doing, you are not doing the right thing."

Sales is not naïve enough to think that there are not some gray courses of action people can take or decisions they can make. But with the right counsel and the right alignment as an organization, you usually make the right decision, he says.

"I can bring my group of ten officers together, and I throw something out in the middle of the room, and just by listening to the debate I think you end up with a black-and-white decision. As an individual, you may not be able to sort it all out yourself. But in an organization, you can figure out any issue if you have openness and open-book management," says Sales.

Despite differing views in some areas, one thing about which all the leaders we interviewed could agree was the need for good advisors, people with integrity. You can't go it alone, says Hank Paulson (Goldman Sachs).

Adds Paulson, "My first rule is, 'Don't be a lone ranger.' Sometimes people are good people but they make judgment errors. It's not a question of morality; they just make a mistake. So whenever there's a close call, you need to seek advice, get a second set of eyes and ears."

Make sure you pick your advisors carefully, he cautions.

"At Goldman Sachs, we have senior people who spend a lot of time on these [gray] issues. We're in a highly regulated industry. It's a lot easier if you're running a company that makes widgets." But, says Paulson, their investment in the effort pays dividends.

Lazarus agrees wholeheartedly. "A lot of it is about transparency—being willing to discuss the difficult parts of an issue [with associates or superiors]," she says. "You need to be willing to talk through the facts. But sometimes, people aren't all that forthcoming with the facts, or a full disclosure of the facts, and that gets people in trouble more than anything."

After you choose a course of action, Lazarus says you must be "willing, with humility, to explain why you chose between two courses of action in a certain way. To be forthcoming [with] the reasoning behind it."

Finally, after you have stated all the facts of the case, have collected opinions from trusted advisors, and believe you can be honest about the decision you will make, you must take time to listen to your own intuitions.

"You have to put some effort into reflection," wrote Badaracco in the *Harvard Management Update* (July 1998). "The Roman emperor Marcus Aurelius, a genuine philosopher-king by any standard, tried once a day to put down all his many cares and burdens and create what he called a 'space of quiet.' The idea is to slow down enough to get a feeling for what your intuitions may be telling you."

The leaders we spoke with would agree with this point. Asking for counsel and taking time for reflection are keys to making the right decision. Other ethical texts suggest putting yourself in the affected party's shoes, to take the proverbial mile walk in their moccasins to see if you would make a different decision. Finally, ask yourself if you would want this decision remembered as part of your personal legacy.

SUMMARY

To have the Integrity Advantage, you do not make tough decisions alone. You ask questions, receive counsel, reflect, and take a long-term view. In short, you ensure that you never make a decision that would violate your internal code of integrity.

Integrity Characteristic #3

YOU MESS UP, YOU 'FESS UP

The first thought as we considered this characteristic was the honesty and openness Johnson & Johnson displayed during the Tylenol poison scare in 1982, when seven people died after using the company's Extra-Strength Tylenol capsules that had been laced with cyanide. The company reacted quickly by alerting the public to the potential danger, ordering its scientists to determine the source of the tampering, recalling millions of the capsules at a cost of around $100 million to the company and replacing them with more tamper-resistant capsules.

Never has a corporation shown such compassion and candidness during such a high-profile and potentially precarious crisis. We were fortunate enough to sit down with Jim Burke in his Manhattan office. Jim was president and CEO of Johnson & Johnson during the Tylenol scare and now serves as the chairman of the Partnership for a Drug Free America.

Burke says the decision to recall millions of bottles of Tylenol worldwide and be unflinchingly open with consumers about the issues surrounding the crisis was a simple decision. Why? Because of the company's history of integrity and strong credo. "And I think that the outcome of that decision was that people increased their trust in Johnson & Johnson," he says.

Burke notes that Johnson & Johnson had a reputation for integrity from the start. But still, the decision to be so honest—and open themselves up to potential crippling legal ramifications—was challenged internally and externally.

"It was a highly controversial decision. People would say, 'You don't have to do that . . . you really don't have to.' Or, 'Why are you doing it?' My argument was, 'I'm leading the company, and I have responsibility to persuade others that we have to do what is in the interest of the values of the company long-term.' "

In the Tylenol case, Burke had the foresight to realize that long-term, the Tylenol brand and the good name of Johnson & Johnson could only survive through open and honest disclosure. "I was also absolutely convinced that an honest approach was going to work, even though I got shaken up a couple of times with people I really cared about who gave me a scenario that suggested it may not."

Critics suggested that a worldwide recall, expressions of sympathy and admissions of process failures would only signal guilt and open a Pandora's box of financial restitution (not to mention the short-term financial cost that would equal around $100 million).

"But in the last analysis, I felt it was the right thing to do, and I also felt the employees of the company would come to the conclusion that it was the right thing to do because it was a value-laden company," says Burke.

The Johnson & Johnson leaders had placed themselves in the right environment. (We'll talk more about environment and culture in the next section.) It was a place where truth was valued as much as profit.

Says Shelly Lazarus (Ogilvy), the leaders at Johnson & Johnson were true to their principles. "I argue that a brand, which is all caught up with the notion of corporate reputation, is the most valuable asset that a company has," Lazarus says. "The better understood your brand is, the more sensitive people are to anything that violates the brand. Given the strength of the J&J brand, had they done anything else, it would have been even more dramatic, because it would have violated a principle by which this company stands and how it is perceived."

Unlike Johnson & Johnson, says the Ogilvy Mather leader, Nike did not stand by its perceived principles when faced with questionable labor practices in Asia in the 1990s.

"Here is a brand that is committed to the highest level of

human endeavor and all sorts of wonderful abstract thoughts. But when it was exposed that they were involved in questionable labor practices, they didn't step up and say, 'It's our responsibility and we are going to do something about this.' Instead, they said, 'We subcontract and that's not our business.' It was a huge disappointment, I think, to their employees and consumers. Because it was so counter to what people saw Nike to stand for."

Says Kent Murdock, president and CEO of the O. C. Tanner Company, a leader in employee-recognition programs and products and the winner of the 2002 American Business Ethics Award, creating a culture of integrity starts with full disclosure—even if the truth is hard to swallow.

"We are honest and candid and timely in our communication to employees," he says. "We don't consider ourselves a paragon of righteousness, but it is our corporate policy to do the right thing and tell the truth—no matter what."

Murdock and the leadership team at O. C. Tanner ensure honest and open communication by holding all-hands meetings with employees at least three times a year and a meeting with all managers once a month, issuing newsletters and videos, and communicating through a strategic performance-recognition program.

The self-deprecating CEO admits it took him a while to figure out the importance of open communication when he first took over as chief executive officer. "I spent the first few years concentrating on budgets and strategy and technology until I realized that the most important thing I and every other leader in North America must do is create the right business culture for employees."

Why? Because the workplace culture touches everything. It mixes into each project. Without being noticed, it becomes a part of all employees.

"If your workplace culture isn't open and honest, it won't create employee satisfaction, and you'll experience turnover and a lack of productivity that will cost you money, ideas and time. On the other hand, if the work environment is ethical, productive and positive, people will stay—and stay committed. They'll drive your company forward," concludes Murdock.

The rewards of an open, positive workplace culture are dramatic. Jeffrey Pfeffer of Stanford University estimates in his book *The Human Equation* that the returns from managing people in ways that build high commitment are typically on the order of 30 percent to 50 percent.

If the rewards are so great, why is integrity missing from

many companies? It's partly a matter of trust, says Wayne Sales (Canadian Tire). A leader has to have enough respect for the intelligence and resilience of his employees and shareholders—and the public—to believe that they can handle the truth, both good and bad.

"You have to think that the average stakeholder can accept the truth. What they cannot accept is dishonesty, breach of integrity, violation of trust. But we see it time and time again," says Sales.

He cites an example of public forgiveness that struck a chord with him while he was working in Detroit. "Chrysler let executives drive their new vehicles. They would turn them in with a few thousand miles on them, but someone was turning back the odometer and selling them as new.

"When this was discovered, I can only imagine what was happening within the organization. The legal counsel was most likely advising, 'You must deny this, you must spin this.' In doing the right thing, Lee Iacocca took out a full-page ad in the *Detroit Free Press* and said, 'Look, we made a mistake. We breached the trust and integrity of our customers. We acknowledge we did this and we promise it will never happen again.' And you know what? Life went on."

If the company had put a marketing spin on the situation,

we might still be talking about it in ethics classes.

Contrast this with Arthur Andersen's approach to its crisis. Today, the Website of this once-trusted giant has been reduced to a few legal statements, one of which read, "Arthur Andersen is planning to appeal the conviction based on flawed jury instructions and erroneous evidentiary rulings that precluded Andersen from presenting its entire defense (June 15, 2002)."

Sounds like a company that has humbly learned its lesson (tongue firmly placed in cheek).

"We saw it with [President] Clinton," adds Sales. "We see it in the marketplace as we speak. Sometimes it's not only what you say but what you don't say that leaves you open in terms of breach of trust and integrity. We saw it in the case of Tylenol that people can handle the truth. Investors can handle the truth."

On this subject, Joe Badaracco (Harvard) says, "If you find yourself being furtive too often—editing a lot of what you say before you say it, or being secretive with documents, hiding them from people—I'd stop and ask what is really going on. It may be time to take a step back and do some reflection" (*Harvard Management Update*, July 1998).

Trusting stakeholders isn't the only barrier to open

communication. Another is lacking faith in yourself. People who feel they have to constantly prove themselves are threatened by mistakes. They can't admit to failure. These people are afraid of being wrong, standing out or disappointing the boss.

Says Frank VanderSloot (Melaleuca), "For people to be totally honest, I think we have to be able to laugh at ourselves and not take ourselves too seriously. If we demand from ourselves perfection, if we never allow ourselves to be imperfect, we are more likely to be dishonest in an effort to protect ourselves from being deemed imperfect."

Sales couldn't agree more. "I just left a quarterly review where we had an individual who came in over budget. But his integrity was not compromised by trying to sweep it under the rug. He made the right decision, even though it came at a high cost to his plan, and probably at the end of the year will cost this individual and members of his team their short-term incentive plan."

Since the individual in question admitted his mistake publicly in Sales's leadership meeting, the executives in the room sat back and clapped. "We literally applauded this individual, because he made the right decision in coming clean about being over plan on expenses," he says.

What about losing his short-term incentive? Didn't having a commitment to integrity hurt the leader in this case? In the short-term, yes, says Sales. The rewards for this leader and his staff will be reaped in the long-term. It's a perspective change. One that all leaders with integrity have to adopt.

"We don't think it is appropriate for individuals to win at any cost. If you are in business long-term, that is absolutely not the path. You must have integrity beyond reproach," said Sales.

Agreed, says Shelly Lazarus. "It's a mundane example of integrity, but if you are not going to make your numbers, please let me know earlier rather than later. We go through so many monthly meetings where people don't 'fess up and admit, 'I'm not going to make that number.' The reason they don't is that they think they are going to be punished. Rather than punishing them at that point, you should laud them in front of others in the company and thank them for their honesty and for giving us the time to make the adjustments to shareholders by the end of year."

"Rewarding those who demonstrate integrity in difficult times is critical," she concludes. "Let them know it is excellent behavior."

Open communication and full disclosure are among leadership's most difficult skills to acquire. The majority of leaders go through their entire career without developing them. The first step is developing a willingness to be wrong—not often—but sometimes, says VanderSloot. "Don't demand that you be right in everything. And know that the public will accept you even more if you make mistakes and are honest about them."

On occasion, Lazarus has heard CEOs, in front of their employees, say 'I made a mistake. I blew that one.' "But it's a very infrequent thing for CEOs to say. But as soon as they say it, it makes everyone in the organization know it's okay to make a mistake. And that creates a very different environment," she continues.

Adds Lazarus, what others won't forgive is a lack of disclosure. "The people who I have trouble dealing with, because I'm not comfortable with them, are people who tend to not give full information," she says. "They purposefully leave out certain parts of the story—they distort facts. The most despicable thing of all to me is they say one thing and do another. That last one is lethal in business. It's not what you say; it's what you do. Most people with integrity are doing more than they are talking."

SUMMARY

To have the Integrity Advantage, you realize that an integral part of leadership is the pursuit of integrity. You are open and honest, disclosing good news and bad. You share all pertinent information, not just that which will help make your case. You acknowledge failure, apologize and make amends.

Integrity Characteristic #4

YOU CREATE A CULTURE OF TRUST

Remember *The Emperor and His New Clothes?* The unfortunate leader unknowingly commissioned unprincipled tailors to sew his robes for a public procession. They made no robes but instead created an ingenious lie: The robes were of so fine a material that only the noblest townspeople would be able to see them.

The emperor was caught. He couldn't see the robes, but admitting he couldn't see them would threaten his noble status. He consulted his closest advisors. Desperate to defend their own nobility, the advisors assured him that they could see the robes—when they truly could not. And so it happened that the unfortunate emperor wore nothing at all in the procession and was publicly humiliated.

The moral of the story? The integrity of the people—and the environment— surrounding you is critical. It may save you from showing up with your moral pants down.

Joe Badaracco (Harvard) explains it this way: "A lot of people who act consistently with integrity do so not just because of who they are, but because of where they are: the people they surround themselves with, the norms of the organization and groups to which they belong. And they should get some credit for being in these situations. They have chosen to work someplace, cultivate friends and join certain organizations, surround themselves with the right people."

Even a person with almost bulletproof integrity never stops needing the support of upright, trustworthy people in an ethical environment.

"If you go back to Aristotle's view, integrity was a matter of character, but you got good character by being part of a good community," says Badaracco. "It wasn't simply like the community was a factory that stamps out people of good character, winds them up and sends them off to wherever they are going. It continued to support and help them and renew them and strengthen them in doing the right thing."

No argument from the leaders we talked to on that point. Environment can make all the difference, and each of the businesspeople we interviewed work tirelessly to create a positive, ethical team environment—not only for themselves but for their employees.

"It's got to start at the top," says Shelly Lazarus (Ogilvy). "If we've learned anything from this current round of revelations, it's that if the people at the top aren't committed to integrity, if they don't live their own values and the values of the company, there's no hope."

She adds that the company's principles must be clear to every employee. People must understand how they will be judged if they fail to live up to those principles.

Then, Lazarus continues, "The company cannot tolerate violations. I come into contact with businesses all the time that tolerate behavior from individuals because they are brilliant or make their numbers. But once others see that it is okay to cheat on the principles, then anything you say from that point forward is meaningless—because the people in the company know you don't mean it."

Says Frank VanderSloot (Melaleuca), "We as managers have a responsibility to not put temptation in front of our employees.

"What if I were to walk through an office and sprinkle $20 bills all around, and asked everyone to not take them? If I came back a week later, I doubt they would all be there, especially if they could be picked up without anyone noticing. The same is true as we handle our business affairs. If we don't have pretty tight controls on our financial affairs, people can be tempted to be dishonest. Without the right environment, people can justify a lot in their minds."

Leadership carries with it a huge burden, says Wayne Sales (Canadian Tire). Not only for your own actions, but often for those in your employ. Sales believes that when people do bad things, it is often leadership's fault. They have created an environment that tolerates wrongdoing overtly or subtly with a wink and a nod.

"Are you saying one thing, but your actions show you turn a blind eye?" asks Sales. "Saying, 'Don't tell me about that decision, I don't want to know.' That sends subtle hints throughout the organization. We think that anything that compromises what you have established in terms of integrity and ethics in your organization will not enable you to survive in the long-term. Because you taint the entire organization by making decisions that are good for the short-term but compromise your ethics."

Sales adds that people with integrity have self-knowledge that keeps them far away from situations where they could be tempted by whatever it is that might corrupt them, making them lose sight of what they really care about.

Consider the story of the wealthy man looking to hire a personal driver. Three candidates were presented with a scenario and asked to answer a question. "Imagine you are driving me to an important speaking engagement. We are late. The shortest route includes a dangerous stretch of road through a winding canyon with a thousand-foot sheer cliff on

• To do all within our power to ensure people (clients, employees, neighbors and suppliers) enjoy every association with O. C. Tanner.

These Decisions help O. C. Tanner hold its moral course in what might otherwise be morally difficult situations. They simplify ethical decision-making. For instance, says Murdock, one of O. C. Tanner's Decisions states that they do not "wink at rule-breakers." When one of the organization's top sales producers was found guilty of sexual harassment, he was terminated. "We followed the Decision without examining the financial consequences," says Murdock.

These Decisions come into play in almost every action taken by O. C. Tanner— including something as straightforward as buying land.

"When we buy a piece of property from an individual, our first priority is to ensure our good name is carried forward," says Murdock. "Thus, we commission an appraisal and then pay more than the appraised price. Our goal is not to be foolish with our money, but to ensure that the name of O. C. Tanner is revered in the community and that we are seen as having the highest degree of integrity in regard to our neighbors."

The list of examples goes on and on. O. C. Tanner recently

spent more than $100,000 on a new water-filtration system when EPA rules changed. "Since we are committed to the well-being of our employees and the community, it was an easy decision. I know that some companies might delay replacing the system until they were legally forced, but an ethical company just makes an ordinary decision to do what is needed or required."

As you examine the actions of O. C. Tanner through the years, a pattern emerges —a pattern established by Decisions made long ago. Making those corporate Decisions was just the first step. The Decisions have to be communicated—and often. And there have to be effective controls in place to correct the course when things veer off track.

At El Paso Corporation, an environment of integrity is enhanced through an Ethics Hotline, a phone number employees can call with any concerns. The employee can either leave his or her name or remain anonymous.

"We have employees questioning why someone got promoted, or perhaps they saw someone from the company out doing something they didn't think was right," says Joel Richards. "We check them all out.

"One example, an employee called and said, 'We have an outside vendor to whom we are giving a lot of business. My understanding is that one of the vendor partners is the brother-in-law of the plant manager where the work is being done.' We checked it out and the employee was right. There was a conflict. It was bad judgment on the manager's part and he was disciplined. We thanked the employee. It was exactly the kind of thing we ought to be examining. We don't find many of the reported items to be actual wrongdoing, but I'm glad employees are watching. I'm glad we encourage this kind of open environment," says Richards.

Of course, you can't create a decision or rule or control for every situation in which an employee may find him or herself. The challenge becomes developing a culture that is based on integrity. That is done most effectively through example.

Says Hank Paulson (Goldman Sachs), leaders must "go below the business principles," attempting to create and maintain an ethical culture through their actions and words.

"Don't assume people know anything. Don't assume that people have the same moral training you have, that they've learned everything you've learned. You've got to reinforce."

Every day, in every way.

Summary

To have the Integrity Advantage, you help to create the right work environment, one that will not test the personal integrity of your employees or coworkers. You reinforce integrity through principles, controls and personal example. And you reward those in your employ who display personal integrity in their actions.

Integrity Characteristic #5

YOU KEEP YOUR WORD

Not too long ago, when you gave your word, it was worth something.

Today, words are cheap.

You'll starve waiting for someone who said "Let's do lunch" to take you out for a meal. "I love you" can mean anything from a profound attachment to simple gratitude, as in "Wow! You fixed my computer! I love you!"

These are lighthearted illustrations of a real problem in business: There simply aren't enough people out there who you can trust. And people don't stay long in organizations devoid of trust. Management researchers James Kouzes and Barry Posner call trust "the most significant predictor of individual satisfaction within [an] organization" (*The Leadership Challenge*, Jossey-Bass, 1997).

Stephen Covey spells it out in his book *Principle-Centered Leadership*. He says that building strong relationships is a key to business success. And, he says, the key to relationships is trust.

Says Hank Paulson (Goldman Sachs), "Every time I get up among our senior people, I tell them Goldman Sachs is a great firm and we're all working to help it and we can all do things to help the company. But the sad truth of the matter is that every one of us has more potential to hurt Goldman Sachs than we have to help it. One mistake in judgment, one dishonorable thing could hurt the firm's reputation. So we've got a business principle that says, 'Our assets are our people, our capital and our reputation.' And if any of those are diminished, the last one is the hardest one to regain. And so, clearly, integrity is just essential, and trust, if you're in our industry."

Jim Burke realized the heightened need for trust when he first arrived at Johnson & Johnson. As a management group, "we understood the value of the (Johnson & Johnson) brand . . . selling it to new mothers." In every action, the company wanted its brand to be a symbol of trust.

Wayne Sales understands that focus. Canadian Tire is an unusual business that Sales says could not run without trust. All of the 451 Canadian Tire stores are owned and operated by associate dealers.

"Our relationship with them, with our customers, with shareholders and with each other as part of the team is built on the foundation of trust, integrity and honesty. It's something that is difficult to earn, easy to lose. And once you lose that air of integrity, it is impossible to regain. It's something you take for granted. Take your children. You love them, but if they breach their integrity, you start to question all they do."

Sales tells the story of an associate dealer who broke the chain of trust. "In our retail business, if we sell merchandise to a customer and it turns out to be defective, the customer returns it to our store and we refund their money."

However, he explains, in many cases, it is simply not cost effective to return defective merchandise to a supplier.

"By the time you pay shipping and handling, [the suppliers] have lost money. So manufacturers give us a refund based on our integrity. We give the customer back her money, we give the store back its money, we file for a refund, and we get our money back from the manufacturer. And we depend on the store to destroy the merchandise."

But Sales discovered a store that was reselling the damaged merchandise at a discount.

"It was a breach of our integrity," explains Sales. "The rest of the organization was looking toward the senior leadership, 'What are you going to do?' We terminated our relationship with this individual. It was a financially tough decision. But I can't underscore enough that every single day people are looking to the leadership of the organization and making mental judgments about their leadership, integrity and their reputation."

How do you recognize a trustworthy person? It's harder than you might think. Maybe it's cynicism. Maybe it's negativism. Whatever the reason, people typically are better at detecting potential scoundrels or people they don't trust than they are at identifying trustworthy individuals.

"Probably for reasons that are evolutionary. A lot of our mental processing is unconscious. And the types of human creatures that survived had early warning systems for reliability and trust that we still possess," Joe Badaracco (Harvard) explains from his office in Cambridge.

But when it got down to it, the leaders we interviewed say that, by and large, following through and doing what you promise is a mark of integrity.

"By trust, I think you are talking about a kind of reliability, which has to do with 'Will they do what they are committed to do, or duty-bound to do?' Before we put our stamp of approval on someone, we have to see and experience a lot," says Badaracco.

Trustworthiness is a unique combination of what you say and what you do, explains Paulson. "It's not just saying the right things, it's doing the right things. It's walking the talk and setting the example."

It's how people learn to trust you, adds Badaracco, "Making good on your commitment is a window on integrity." As long as, he points out, you don't become so rigidly oriented toward doing your duty that you become an automaton, unable to think for yourself. "You wonder how these people will handle themselves in more complicated situations."

For many of the leaders we interviewed, being described as trustworthy was one of the highest compliments they could receive.

"For me, I'd rather be trusted than loved, I guess," says Jim Burke (Johnson & Johnson). "And I think it's easier to love somebody that you trust. It's certainly easier to do business with them."

He adds, "A person with integrity clearly is someone you trust. Trust is a very, very good word."

"The more people trust you, the more they think of you. Trust is a synonym for having enormous respect for somebody," Burke continues.

You can't go wrong by wanting and working to become more trustworthy. People who do so come out ahead in business and in life.

"I think that you could argue that trust is the name of the game, and if you're trusted, you're winning the game," says Millard Fuller (Habitat for Humanity). "You don't hear it too often, but it is a very valuable asset to have people say about you: 'Well, one thing you can do is trust so-and-so if he says such-and-such.'"

Says Burke, "The bottom line is that ethical behavior should be a route toward gaining the trust of people for whom you feel responsible."

What a wonderful statement by a wonderful leader. It bears repeating. We act with integrity so that we can gain the trust of those for whom we are responsible. And there are many: our employees, our families, our coworkers, our friends, and our employers.

Fuller says the man in life he most trusted was his spiritual mentor, Clarence Jordan.

"He had more integrity than anybody I knew. He had an amazing way to see things and articulate things."

Jordan won the trust of people such as Fuller through his ethical behavior. In the 1950s, Jordan was the leader of an integrated Christian community, Koinonia Farm, located near Americus, Georgia. The community was heavily persecuted.

Members were beaten and their buildings were burned and destroyed. The local white business establishment boycotted the community.

"Clarence tried to buy chicken feed. The guy told him to get out of town, called him a 'nigger-loving communist,' " recalls Fuller. "Clarence turned to leave, but the man then said, 'Wait a second. I'll sell you anything you want if you'll renounce your views on integration in the paper through an ad.' Clarence responded, 'There's been a misunderstanding. I just came in to get a bag of seed. My soul is not for sale.' "

SUMMARY

Employees don't follow leaders they don't trust. Employers don't hire people or promote employees they don't trust. Clients don't buy from suppliers they don't trust. To have the Integrity Advantage, you act with integrity to gain trust.

Integrity Characteristic #6

You Care About the Greater Good

Some people call it karma. Some call it the Golden Rule. The concept remains the same: What goes around comes around.

Even today, in the technological, hectic, driven twenty-first century, this ancient truth has validity. It is not naïve to think that you should look out for the organization to which you belong, care about the products and services you produce, and watch out for your teammates and employees. In turn, you will gain a greater sense of purpose and peace in your life.

Okay, a few of you just snickered. Maybe you have had the boss from Hades, or worked in the cubicle next to the coworker who got promoted because he stole all your best ideas, or sat down the hall from Shirley who worked thirty years for the company only to be laid off a year before retirement.

"I have to look out for myself," you're saying.

There are a fair share of demagogues and abusers out there. But if you are committed to your organization and what you sell or deliver to consumers, and if you make decisions that benefit your teammates (even above your own gain), you will be viewed as a person of integrity, and you will succeed in the long-term. Most importantly, you'll feel a great sense of accomplishment. But if based on your body of accumulated knowledge you still don't believe that companies take care of their most committed, ethical people, there is a very good chance that you have been working in an ethically diseased environment.

Wayne Sales's company, Canadian Tire, is Canada's most-shopped retailer. The company was voted Canada's Best Employer by that country's national paper, *The Globe and Mail*, so Sales should know a thing or two about creating positive work environments. According to him, personal integrity is not only noticed at his company but also rewarded. The most obvious characteristic of a person with integrity is a degree of selflessness, he adds.

"One of the most important questions we ask about people in our organization is, 'What is driving them?' Is it personal gain or the welfare of the customer, shareholders and the organization at large? It is very evident in a person's behavior. For example, we had an individual who came on board. Through some actions he took, it became very clear, very early in his career, that he was much more concerned about his own financial well-being than our stakeholders'."

At the O. C. Tanner Company, Kent Murdock calls it "commitment to the collective whole."

"There is a huge ethical perspective from committing to bettering the company versus a personal agenda of how much money can I get out of here," says Murdock. "I'm not saying you have to sacrifice for the company—work eighty hours a week or give up your family. But to be successful long-term, and to be noticed and rewarded, you must ensure that all your actions will make the company successful. That mind-set will not only keep you out of trouble but give you the esteem of your leaders and coworkers. You will lose yourself in your work. And, as [Saint] Matthew tells us, by losing yourself you will find yourself."

We recognize that this Integrity Advantage may sound idealistic. After all, won't an attitude of devotion simply get you taken advantage of?

Not so, says Millard Fuller (Habitat For Humanity). He says a person with integrity lives with humility and an eye toward others, and can still be successful and well rewarded. A person with integrity is typically a much better leader than a selfish type. He summarizes that, "Integrity is thinking of the bigger picture, finding a purpose that is bigger than yourself."

Says Jorge Paulo Lemann (Gillette), ethics are different around the world. But, he says, one thing that remains constant: A person with integrity has the utmost respect for his or her teammates.

"No matter where you are in the world, you treat other people exactly how you would like to be treated—honestly and fairly," says Lemann.

For Shelly Lazarus (Ogilvy), that kind of respect means being brutally honest with your teammates and employees when necessary.

"One of the real failings of certain well-intended people in business, and a violation of principles of integrity, is when bosses don't let employees know where they really stand in an organization, how they are doing. These bosses don't want to hurt the employee's feelings, so they are supportive and only say nice things. Then these employees get to a point in their careers where it is clear that they are not making a contribution and they are not growing.

"I don't think you can do a greater disservice to someone who works for you or with you than to not be truthful about performance."

In short, a person with integrity never takes the easy out.

SUMMARY

To have the Integrity Advantage, you are deeply committed to and make decisions that will benefit the entire organization to which you belong. You care passionately about your company, products and services, and especially your teammates. Through your work, you gain a sense of deeper purpose.

Integrity Characteristic #7

You're Honest but Modest

If you've ever told someone how honest you are then you probably told a lie.

Honesty isn't something you claim, like a fancy title. It's a judgment made by the people around you based on your actions, every day of your life.

"People who talk about their own integrity usually put me on alert," says Shelly Lazarus (Ogilvy). "It's been my experience that people tend to live their lives in a certain way. And those who are honest wouldn't know how to be dishonest if you asked them to."

"I had a spokesperson once who was out touting us—and telling our salespeople to tout us—as an honest company . . . and to really go into our honesty as a company," Frank VanderSloot (Melaleuca) tells us, shaking his head. "I reeled him in and those he had talked to. I told them it's not the right thing to do, first. And second, we would like to run a business where, after someone has had experience with us for five or ten or fifteen years, they say for themselves, 'That's an honest outfit.' We want to be worthy of that. And our intention is to have people say it about us, without us having to say it."

The same is true with an individual.

Says Joe Badaracco (Harvard), people with integrity often move patiently, carefully and quietly. "They don't spearhead large-scale ethical crusades. They right—or prevent—moral wrongs in the workplace inconspicuously and usually without casualties. I have come to call these people quiet leaders because their modesty and restraint are in large measure responsible for their extraordinary achievements" (*Harvard Business Review*, September 2001).

Humble, quiet leaders are also considerate and courteous. They do the little things that win friends and admirers. They smile and greet coworkers every day, they reflect on how their decisions will affect others, they praise and recognize their employees and even their bosses, they control their tempers, and they allow others to be kind to them.

In other words, they act like their moms taught them to all those years ago.

SUMMARY

To have the Integrity Advantage, you do not proclaim your virtue or honesty. That's like boasting of your humility. You allow your actions to speak louder than your words.

Integrity Characteristic #8

You Act Like You're Being Watched

Does it seem as if your every move is watched? As if someone is carefully observing your actions, scrutinizing your words and analyzing your motives?

If so, you're not crazy. You're a leader. (Although some might claim there's a fine line between the two.) People really are watching you. A leader with integrity knows this and makes decisions that can be scrutinized by anyone. Even their mothers.

Says Hank Paulson (Goldman Sachs), "So often we have a set of rules and then the goalposts move and society changes. We've got to be asking ourselves all the time not only what the rules are but is this right? How would this practice look if it were written up on the front page of the *New York Times*? Even if everybody in the industry does it."

Don Graham (*Washington Post*) has closely observed one man for the better part of thirty years. That mentor is Warren Buffett, CEO of Berkshire Hathaway. After all those years—encompassing thousands of business decisions—Graham believes Buffett is one of the greatest exemplars of integrity in business that he has ever known. He says Buffett makes decisions as if one of his investors was constantly peering over his shoulder, and he isn't afraid to openly discuss any and all decisions.

"I think it's worth studying every aspect of Berkshire Hathaway's behavior, because in things big and small it is an organization—and a man—that sets the standard for running a company with high integrity," says Graham.

For example, he says, "Warren famously writes his own annual reports. They are unusual in a number of ways. First, they are very readable. Second, they are actually written by the CEO. But perhaps they are most unusual in that they tell both the good and bad news about that company. If a business is going poorly, if they made a poor acquisition, if they made a financial decision that didn't work out, Warren will tell the story and describe why it didn't work out. In many cases he'll put the blame on himself, even if it doesn't necessarily belong there."

While every company claims it is run for the benefit of the shareholders, at the end of every Berkshire Hathaway Annual Report is a statement of what Buffett and his right-hand man, Charlie Munger, refer to as Owner-Related Business Principles. The principles outline in specific detail how the company will deal with its stockholders. Berkshire Hathaway shareholders are treated like trusted partners. Shareholders are dealt with honestly, as Buffett and Munger say they would want to be treated if they were minority partners.

A point made by almost every leader we talked to: This principle, 'You Act Like You're Being Watched,' should be taught first and foremost in the home. But, they say, many parents don't understand how to rear children with long-term integrity, who make the right decisions when faced with tough choices, who will not buckle under pressure.

The key is personal example, says Millard Fuller (Habitat for Humanity) "Parents can teach it, but they must teach it by example. Children notice behavior a whole lot more than they notice words. They notice if a clerk gives you the wrong change and Dad walks away and says, 'Look that clerk gave me $5 too much; I'm lucky.' "

As a boy, Frank VanderSloot (Melaleuca) doesn't remember his father ever saying a word about integrity. "But I never saw him tell a lie. And I never saw him exaggerate. That had a big impact on me. But I've also been around people who really touted themselves as being honest and ethical. And, without exception, they were trying to convince themselves as much as someone else that they were honest."

Like most of the leaders with whom we talked, Hank Paulson (Goldman Sachs) has a basic belief that people are inherently good, but their upbringing either enhances and brings out that goodness, or, sadly, suppresses it. "I have no doubt that the best and easiest way to learn how to be a person of integrity is when you're very young in your home, from your role models. That's not always possible. My wife spends a lot of time in the inner-city schools and we work with a lot of kids who may need to learn what integrity means later in life."

What if, upon honest reflection, you find that your innate goodness turns out to be more on the suppressed side? The key is finding a mentor. Someone like Buffett is to Graham.

"I think you can learn. These values can be reinforced with one mentor or another. Sometimes it's a teacher early in school, sometimes it's a coach. By the time you get to business school or into business, it's a little bit more difficult if you don't have some of the basic values or codes of conduct. But even there, I think [leaders] can make a difference and teach you," says Paulson.

The sooner you start—the better.

Paulson acknowledges that he likes people to join Goldman Sachs early in their careers. "Our culture works better when we can hire them and have them stay throughout their career so that we can teach them our values. I believe people are innately good, are innately attracted to good, but they need role models and teaching, and the earlier that that can happen in your life and career the better off you are."

SUMMARY

To have the Integrity Advantage, you assume your every move is being watched. You ensure that your integrity is passed along to future generations through your example.

Integrity Characteristic #9

YOU HIRE INTEGRITY

A news story reported about a migrant worker who found a bag of cash on the street. Without pause, he turned it over to the authorities—only to have many of his friends call him a fool.

We'd call him the perfect employee.

Here's why. It's relatively easy to teach telephone etiquette, computer skills or company procedures. Even communication or language barriers can be overcome. But it is very difficult to train a person to have integrity.

Please don't misunderstand us; we're not saying it's impossible. We just discussed how it's possible to learn or enhance integrity at any age. But that journey is very personal, very individual. An outside force, such as an employer, can't prescribe it. It's not something that happens overnight. That's one reason Don Graham (*Washington Post*), recommends hiring and promoting people from inside your organization when possible.

"There's a very good reason for concentrating your hires and promotions on people who already work in your organization. The best way to predict what someone's going to do in the future is to know what they've done in the past—watch how people address difficult business issues, how they deal with the people who work for them, how they deal with the people for whom they work. You may be able to put on a certain face for a day or even a week, but you're not going to be able to hide the person you are for five or ten years."

Graham tells a story about Frank Batten, who for years ran Landmark Communications and founded the Weather Channel. "Frank is a person of total integrity," says Graham. "Frank once said, 'When you go outside for hire you always get a surprise. Sometimes it's a good surprise. But you never hire quite the person you thought you were hiring.' "

Ask yourself honestly: What do you usually look for in a job applicant? Years of experience? College degree? Specific skill sets?

Jorge Paulo Lemann (Gillette) says integrity is the first thing he looks for in a candidate. "I've dealt with a lot of different people . . . Europeans, Brazilians . . . different religions, different backgrounds. I really don't care. I think the one trait that you really can't deal with is a lack of integrity. If a person is playing games, even if they are useful to the firm in some ways, in the end they get mixed up; they don't function within the whole organization.

"If a person is bad tempered, nervous, I don't care. As long as he has integrity you can deal with him, with any problem. The whole organization will function much better if people have integrity overall. Good and ethical people attract more good and ethical people."

Years ago, Warren Buffett was asked to help choose the next CEO for Salomon Brothers, says Don Graham. "What do you think [Warren] was looking for? Character and integrity—more than even a particular background. When the reputation of the firm is on the line every day, character counts," says Graham.

For busy leaders, who can't afford unpleasant surprises in their new employees, there is an answer: integrity. It's the single most effective way to ensure a good fit with the people you hire. Does that mean that nothing else matters? No. It does mean that character is something you actively evaluate and consider in all new hires, despite the difficulty in doing so.

"What we look for are people who understand that the ends do not justify the means. I tell people, 'If you really feel like something is wrong, we expect you to voice your concerns.' We need to do everything in an appropriate and legal manner," says Joel Richards (El Paso Corporation).

At the first sign that an employee might develop into a

leader, Richards is carefully watching. "I want to know how people feel about the rules. We are real sticklers for following the rules, even little things like expense reports. You learn a lot about people from their expense reports."

What about violators who are caught cheating—for example, when an employee records a business meal on an expense report when it is clear he or she is not traveling? "When confronted, the employee always comes up with some justification. But we just can't put up with it," says Richards. "If you can't trust an employee to be truthful on an expense report, if you can't trust them with small dollars, how can you trust them with making decisions involving millions of dollars?"

To avoid these problems, Richards strives to hire and promote people who have a strong ethical core, who will not be tempted by misguided voices around them, and who are willing to take a stand if they ever discover wrongdoing in their company.

Speaking up can be a very hard decision, and even harder to actually do. But staying quiet can be costlier in the long run. As the character Jean Valjean sings in the Broadway version of *Les Misérables*, "If I speak, I am condemned. If I stay silent, I am damned." People with an ethical core answer to a higher law.

And it seems that they are in demand in the workplace. The New York Times Job Market research team found that ethics have become more important in the recruitment process in the post-Enron work environment. It seems that today, managers doing the hiring are much more likely to emphasize and look for integrity characteristics during recruitment (*HR Fact Finder*, July 2002).

Not surprising, considering the growing number of world-wide brands and reputations that have been destroyed by the unethical actions of a handful of individuals without integrity.

SUMMARY

To have the Integrity Advantage, you hire and surround yourself with straight arrows who have a strong sense of personal integrity. You promote those who demonstrate an ability to be trusted.

Integrity Characteristic #10

You Stay the Course

McDonald's has experienced great long-term success in the fast-food industry. The company owes that to its consistency.

It's not the secret sauce, the food, the clean stores or the fabulous marketing campaigns. They all are part of McDonald's magic formula. But the real, underlying strength of the McDonald's brand rests in its consistency among its locations. From Hong Kong to Wisconsin, when you pull into the Double Arches, you know exactly what you're going to get.

Consistency pays off on a personal level, too. First, because it's very hard to find. Second, because people who demonstrate consistency are absolutely real. What you see is what you get.

Says Diane Peck (Safeway), "People who have integrity are consistent in what they say and do. They are almost predictable. I once worked for a person who had a level of integrity that I really respected. . . . I knew how he would react in most any situation. People with integrity have this consistency, this predictability, this believability. You know what to expect with them, you know what the outcome is going to be. You put the pieces together over time as you watch a person behave and react to things."

The hard part is, like love, you can't hurry consistency. It's proven over time. If you remember the words of Don Graham *(Washington Post)*, "You may be able to show a certain face for a day, or even a week. But you're not going to be able to be other than the person you are for five or ten years."

Jorge Paulo Lemann (Gillette) remembers his friend Sam Walton, founder of the Wal-Mart empire, as not only honest and ethical, but a man of consistency.

Says Lemann, "I was with Sam once. We were in a competitor's store. I had a bad cold, and in the store I saw a flask of Vicks Vapor Rub. I was there, I saw it and so I bought it. It cost twenty-five cents or something like that. I paid at the counter and Sam was absolutely furious. He went berserk. He made me go back and get a refund. Then we immediately went to a Wal-Mart store where he showed me that the same product cost one cent less. He could not understand why I would buy something in a competitor's store that cost one cent more."

Says Lemann, Walton believed it was his duty to provide the lowest prices to his consumers. That was a core principle. And he stuck to his principles—consistently.

Lemann adds that people with consistency "are very much to the point. They are very confident about saying what they believe. There's not much b.s. They're courageous. It saves a lot of time and is a good practice."

Consistency is the mark of a person who is not impacted by changes outside him. Money, power, influence may come and go, but a person's actions are inseparably connected to his or her inner moral values.

Some might argue that you can't truly harness the Integrity Advantage without developing consistency. They'd be absolutely right.

SUMMARY

To have the Integrity Advantage, you have ethical consistency and predictability. Your life demonstrates wholeness and harmony between your values and your actions.

Summary: You Can Take It With You

A clergyman reminded a rich old miser who was on his deathbed that he couldn't take his riches with him. "Then I'm not going!" the cantankerous man replied.

Integrity is one of the few things in life you can take with you, wherever you go. It becomes a part of you and sticks with you through economic downturns just as it does in the good times. It's something no one can take away from you.

"On a personal level, integrity is its own reward," says Hank Paulson (Goldman Sachs). "At the end of the day, the only real satisfaction that comes is from doing good. People like working hard toward a goal and feel satisfaction when they make progress toward that goal. But the goal has to be for good. No one is happy with him or herself if they're not a good person."

That's the core benefit of integrity. For the lucky among us, it's enough. For the rest of us, it's comforting to know that integrity has tangible benefits, as well.

"It absolutely pays," says Shelly Lazarus (Ogilvy) "for a lot of reasons. If you are going to run an organization of people, you have to instill and inspire in people a sense of belief in what the company stands for. There has to be consistency in behavior and outlook. To gain the belief and loyalty of a group of people, there has to be a core set of principles that one is true to. Otherwise, it's very hard to build a bond with your people."

"Integrity is a competitive advantage," says Wayne Sales. (Canadian Tire). "And as proof of that, we have been voted the best company in all of Canada in which to work. When we interview people today, you get the immediate sense that people just want to be part of this organization, even though we put them through heck in terms of the interview process—because 'fit' in the organization is very important."

The unusually rigorous interview process at Canadian Tire doesn't seem to drive people away. Just the opposite. Sales did not use a recruiter for the last three executive appointments to his team. "I had phone call after phone call from people wanting to join our team."

What draws people to Sales's organization? Integrity in its culture and in its people.

As we said, integrity truly is a competitive advantage—in business and in life.

Part Three

Taking Stock of Where You Stand

Individual integrity is proven in those moments when we choose to do what's right, no matter what we might gain or lose: popular opinion, fortune, fame or power. For most of us, thankfully, those are private moments. For some, they play out on the world stage.

Katharine "Kay" Graham was CEO of the *Washington Post* for twenty-eight years, and for almost all that time she was the only woman running a Fortune 1000 company.

"She was the exemplar of integrity within this company," says Don Graham, her son and current CEO of the *Post*. "And her defining moment, no question about it, was her decision to publish the Pentagon Papers."

The Pentagon Papers was a classified report requested by Secretary of Defense Robert McNamara on the origins and history of the United States' involvement in the war in Vietnam. One of the report's authors, Daniel Ellsburg, gave a copy to the *New York Times*, which—with great secrecy—had written news stories describing the content.

After publishing stories for several days, the paper was enjoined under a court order. The *Times* quickly appealed, but the U.S. Circuit Court of Appeals in New York upheld the order, effectively halting the *Times* from publishing any more information based on the Pentagon Papers until the courts had an opportunity to review the content.

Ellsburg then approached a *Washington Post* editor with a copy of the Papers. Reporters and editors gathered in Executive Editor Ben Bradlee's living room and started reading and developing stories based on the report. Within hours, Katharine Graham was embroiled in controversy.

Says Don Graham, "The reporters and editors and Bradlee were telling her, 'We must publish a story based on these papers. It's overwhelmingly in the public interest. It's important. The war is the biggest news story today, and this report bears directly on why we got into it. And we can do it in a way that there's no compromise to national security.' "

At the same time, Katharine Graham's lawyers were warning of the inherent risks of publishing material that the *Times* had been ordered to stop printing.

Outside pressures were mounting, as well. The U.S. deputy attorney general sent a warning to Graham that a company convicted of a felony (in this case, a violation of the Espionage Act) could not own television stations. "Television stations were absolutely crucial to our corporation at that time," says Don Graham.

There was one more important fact for Katharine Graham to consider: The *Post* was selling its stock on Wall Street for the first time that week.

Faced with seemingly irreconcilable ideological, financial and legal conflicts, Katharine Graham followed the course that was in alignment with her promises to herself, the *Post* and the public—and published.

"The risks were considerable, but the newspaper had a stated goal of being the best it could possibly be," says Don Graham. "There was no question about the importance of the story, its importance to the public. Yet it wasn't a story that would sell more newspapers; it was a story that was important public information. It was a decision made with complete integrity. It was a case of living by your goals. It certainly is the iconic example of the *Washington Post*."

Katharine Graham made the right decision for her organization. The Supreme Court of the United States ultimately upheld her decision. In the long run, Katharine Graham's tough choice bolstered the *Post*'s reputation as one of the nation's foremost newspapers. In fact, in recounting the growth of that newspaper, the *Post*'s executive editor put the greatest emphasis not on its Watergate coverage but on the decision to publish the Pentagon Papers.

Graham's decision fulfilled a trust that was implicit between readers and the *Post:* to print the truth, regardless of the financial risks to the owners.

Readers also expect the press to ensure that reported information is accurate and truthful. Don Graham gives a more recent example of an act of integrity where a publication chose not to publish.

In the late 1990s, Rick Smith was chairman and editor in chief of *Newsweek*. It was a *Newsweek* reporter who first learned from Linda Tripp of the relationship between White House intern Monica Lewinsky and President Clinton. It was not only a sensational scoop, but it was a story Smith knew would garner international attention. Unlike the Pentagon Papers, this story would sell newsstand copies of *Newsweek*. In fact, they would most likely be pulled off the rack in record numbers. But Rick was in a quandary. The information was delivered to him on a Friday. *Newsweek* has to be edited and put to press by day's end on Saturday.

He looked at the story. At that point, it had only one source: Linda Tripp. The reporter had been unable to talk to Monica Lewinsky or anyone representing her, as that day she was making her first contact with investigators. The reporter had also been unable to talk to the White House, as that day

President Clinton was giving a deposition in the Paula Jones case. No one had reached Vernon Jordan, another major character in the story, for comment. The writer had heard part of one of the tapes that Tripp had made of Lewinsky but didn't have the tape in hand.

"They had Linda Tripp's side of the story. . . . What she had brought to *Newsweek* was an account of questionable conduct by Monica Lewinsky and President Clinton. But they had not completed the reporting because neither [Lewinsky nor President Clinton] had any opportunity to respond. And in the book of any journalist, you do not print very serious allegations of misconduct without giving the person accused an opportunity to reply," says Graham.

Smith evaluated where *Newsweek* stood and made the decision not to print the story in that issue.

"He didn't print anything because there wasn't a corner of these allegations where they had a complete story. [Smith] made the decision that the reporting on the story was incomplete, even though he knew that *Newsweek* wouldn't get sole credit for breaking the story," says Graham.

"Again, to me, that was a highly, highly principled decision—a sensational decision. Smith knew that this story was certain to appear in some newspaper or publication during the following week. In fact, it was the *Washington Post* that first broke it a couple of days later, although not based on any information provided by *Newsweek*."

As soon as the *Post* broke the story, *Newsweek* posted its information on its Website. *Newsweek* continued to lead the coverage of the story, and broke most of the major developments from then on. This was a case of a story that would have sold a lot of copies of the magazine. It was a story involving sex and the highest levels of power. It certainly cost *Newsweek* to hold the story, but, says Graham, "It was a decision made with integrity that will benefit the magazine in the long-term."

The ability to make the right decision under pressure shows real integrity. Have you got what it takes?

In the next few pages, you will be asked a series of questions designed to help you gauge your own integrity level and begin to take steps to enhance it. But beware: While your experience won't be as public as the accounts you have just read, it may be equally difficult and—if undertaken with the right attitude— just as inspiring.

To gain the Integrity Advantage, we suggest you follow four steps:

Step One: Call a Personal Time Out

Step Two: Get a Second Opinion . . . and a Third

Step Three: Evaluate Your Environment

Step Four: Start an Individual Revolution

Step 1:

CALL A PERSONAL TIME OUT

It's time now to stop.

That's right, stop. Stop racing around. Stop answering the phone. Stop worrying about the most recent crisis at work. Find an hour of undisrupted time for some serious self-evaluation. It helps if things are quiet. It helps if you can be alone. It helps if you don't feel rushed.

Finding an oasis of personal time may possibly be one of the greatest challenges of this book; but it's also one of the most important.

Remember Joe Badaracco's words: "You have to put some effort into reflection." He told the story of the Roman emperor Marcus Aurelius who once a day put away the many worries of his leadership to create what he called a "space of quiet." Says the Harvard professor, "The idea is to slow down enough to get a feeling for what your intuitions may be telling you."

The critical first step is to determine where you now stand. Take some time by yourself, take out a journal or a notebook, find a pen and settle in.

Your assignment: Using the Ten Characteristics of Integrity from part 2, rate yourself from 1 to 10 (10 being the highest) in each area. Jot down at least two specific reasons for your assessment in each area.

1. You know that little things count.
2. You find the white (when others see gray).
3. You mess up, you 'fess up.
4. You create a culture of trust.
5. You keep your word.
6. You care about the greater good.
7. You're honest but modest.
8. You act like you're being watched.
9. You hire integrity.
10. You stay the course.

NOTE: Do this with paper and pen. You will need your evaluations later; and no matter how sharp your memory is, you won't remember all of your first impressions.

In the novel *Pride and Prejudice* by Jane Austen, the character Elizabeth exclaims, "Until this moment, I never knew myself!" You may experience a similar epiphany during this short exercise.

The next step will help ensure that you enjoy the acquaintance.

Step Two

GET A SECOND OPINION... AND A THIRD

Charles Handy, Irish-born social philosopher, influential management guru and innovative thinker, is famous for beginning his seminars and speeches with this question: "Whom do you really trust? Write them down and count them up."

"[Handy] said it was amazing how small that number was," says Joe Badaracco (Harvard). "It almost never got over fifty. It was often two, three, five or ten. Which is to say that you need to be very careful in your judgment of who you trust and who you don't."

It also makes one wonder about the correlation between being trustworthy and trusting others. It has been said that trust breeds trust and that those who do not easily trust others do so because they subconsciously understand that they are not trustworthy. We neither support nor refute this hypothesis, but we do agree that a "trust inventory," as Handy has suggested, will help determine your integrity level.

Write down the name of every person on this planet you trust implicitly and totally. Think about this carefully and take your time. Who would you call first in a major crisis that required significant financial or emotional assistance? Who do you trust to never take advantage of you, even when you are the most vulnerable? Who would you trust to guide you through a challenging decision?

Is your list short? Look at it again and add to it. Are there any others you have not thought of? Former teachers, friends, relatives, coworkers, bosses? Or did you add names to the list to make yourself feel like you are above the norm?

Your next assignment is to contact the people on your list and seek integrity feedback from them. This will require some courage. Start with the top three people. Let them know that you have read this book and that it has compelled you to make a conscious effort to increase your long-term personal integrity and trustworthiness. Introduce them to the Ten Characteristics of Integrity and ask them to help you determine which characteristics are your strengths and which are your weaknesses. Ask them for complete honesty and guarantee to them that the candor with which they respond will not adversely affect your relationship.

Keeping your promise to not become offended will be on its own a test of your integrity.

Hank Paulson (Goldman Sachs) says that how others perceive you is key if you want to build your level of trustworthiness. "Trust is established through action and over time, and it is a leader's responsibility to demonstrate what it means to keep your word and earn a reputation for trustworthiness."

Keep Paulson's words in mind as you gather feedback and take ample time to review it. You may check back with your trusted parties for clarification, but do not argue or debate their comments. (Remember, you gave your personal guarantee not to become offended.) Decide if you would like to contact additional people from your list.

The information you obtain is important. You now have a great deal of your personal reputation written on paper and categorized. It was given to you by people whom you trust, who are interested in helping you reach your goals. This is a valuable asset and an important step in the right direction. You are now prepared to move to step three: Evaluate Your Environment.

Step Three

EVALUATE YOUR ENVIRONMENT

If morally ill people surround you, it can be hard for you to get better. Before you set your goals, take time to evaluate the ethical health of organizations in which you participate. Let's start with your employer.

Don't rely on the mission statement to represent your company's values. The truth is that most companies in North America profess to behave with corporate integrity. It is quite common for any corporate mission statement in any industry to emphasize integrity and ethical behavior as values held near and dear to the company. The sayings line the entryway walls of businesses from coast to coast. But when a lack of integrity occurs, leaders openly wonder why the rank and file doesn't follow their profound proclamations—why they continue to pilfer pens from office supplies, why they pad their expense accounts with a few more bucks every month, and why they try to get away with little things that add up to so much.

Ask yourself these questions:

1. Is there an unreasonably high focus on the company stock price as opposed to creating long-term value for stakeholders?

2. Are employees routinely exposed to ethical temptation, or are safeguards in place to keep honest people honest?

3. Is company communication frequent, open and honest? Or is information shared strictly on a need-to-know basis?

4. Is it okay to admit you've made a mistake? Can you recall your company or supervisor publicly admitting an error?

5. Have you ever been asked to violate your personal ethical standards in the name of the company (e.g., erasing e-mails, misrepresenting company services or profits, lying to an outside party)?

6. What happens when an employee breaks a rule or does something dishonest? Does your company wink at rule-breakers who are successful?

7. Does your organization pay its bills on time and in full?

8. Is everyone held to the same standard or are there discrepancies?

9. Is there at least one person at your company who is of high enough integrity to be considered a mentor?

10. Do you trust your immediate supervisors? What about upper-management?

11. Have you ever caught your leaders in a lie?

12. Are integrity and character formally considered in hiring decisions? Is honesty rewarded in the promotion process?

13. Would you enjoy staying with this organization for the long-term?

14. Are you proud to tell your friends, family and acquaintances where you work? What is their reaction when you mention the company?

Trust your own eyes, ears and brain to help you understand the integrity level of your company. Trust what you have experienced. Mentally filed away are clear pictures of company decisions and the processes used to reach those decisions.

Hopefully, your evaluation reveals an organization that values integrity and has a consistent system to reward and reinforce it. But you might find yourself in an organization with a philosophy that Diane Peck (Safeway) describes as, "do whatever it takes, push the envelope, look the other way, we've got to make our numbers."

In those circumstances, your choices are threefold, she says. "You either go along to get along, try to change the way things are done, or part company."

For the person truly committed to harnessing the Integrity Advantage, your options narrow to two:

1. Work to change the environment. (This is most effective if you are in a position of influence.)

2. Get out of Dodge.

What about sticking around and toughing it out? Chances are, you won't come out of it unscathed. In ninety-nine cases out of a hundred, either you go or your integrity goes. It's a law almost as certain as the Law of Gravity. On the other hand, the act of surrounding yourself with people of integrity will raise your integrity level a few notches.

Take Canadian Tire as a positive example. Says CEO Wayne Sales, in that company, "integrity goes to our statement of purpose, why we exist as an organization. We exist to serve and enrich the lives of customers, shareholders, our teams and our communities. That begins to describe not only who we are but the kind of culture we want in our organization. The word *trustworthy* is central to what we hope to achieve. It deals with: Can I count on you, can you count on me? It speaks to the heart of integrity. Can you trust me to do the right thing, to make the right decision for the right reasons for this organization?"

Work isn't the only organization to which you belong. Most of us belong to many—family, social, sporting, religious, political. Evaluate these organizations as you do your work, using the previous list and the Ten Characteristics of Integrity from part 2.

Look at little things. Do people you consider to be your friends cheat on their taxes and brag about it or steal from their employer? In your family, do you support your children in lying to their teachers about tardiness or absences? Integrity is as critical in these relationships as in your work organization.

"You can't have success without trust," says Jim Burke (Johnson & Johnson). "How many marriages do you know where there is a lack of trust that have been successful? Marriage is built on trust. Friendships are built on trust. I think we've lost sight of that. That's what all the commotion is all about today, a loss of trust."

Sounds like the perfect time for a revolution.

Step Four

START AN INDIVIDUAL REVOLUTION

You've heard the saying "Some things never change."

The truth is that most things never change unless we put forth some effort. Change requires momentum. That momentum has to come from inside of you.

If you're like most people, you've come up with a long list of things you'd like to change. That's great. It shows you're thinking about integrity. But don't try to accomplish them all at once.

Instead, choose just two. One should be something you will do differently. The other should be something you won't do anymore. For example, a list might look like this:

1. I will complete my assignments on deadline and be true to my word.

2. I won't ignore e-mail or phone mail messages.

Try to choose situations that occur frequently, so that you are often reminded of your desire to increase your integrity. Keep each goal manageable (in this case, bigger isn't better.) so that you can succeed. Choose goals that are specific, not general. For example, a goal like, "I won't lie at work," is harder to fulfill than one that specifies, "I won't lie on my time card," or "I won't use sick days when I'm not sick."

Concentrate on these goals for one week, then select two more. Work on those as you continue the behaviors you have already mastered.

This can be learned, says Hank Paulson (Goldman Sachs). "I have a basic belief that every man and woman is inherently good, and that they have an infinite capacity to reflect that goodness. Of course, the best and certainly the easiest time to learn how to manifest those qualities is as a child, at home, from family role models. But not everyone has that early opportunity, and many people must learn these lessons later in life. The point is that they can and they do."

Whether your integrity is high now, or in need of some attention, the good news is that we can all enhance our attention to this vital business principle. As a character in the film *The Princess Diaries* says, "From now on you'll be traveling the road between who you think you are and who you can be. The key is to allow yourself to make the journey."

Focus on the behaviors, two at a time, and you'll be on your way to making the Integrity Advantage your advantage.

When All Is Said and Done

At the end of the day, people with integrity have one thing in common, says Don Graham (*Washington Post*): They sleep well.

He keeps that thought in mind when faced with an ethical dilemma. Recalls Graham, "Warren Buffett once said to a business school class, 'I cannot tell you that honesty is the best policy. I can't tell you that if you behave with perfect honesty and integrity somebody somewhere won't behave the other way and make more money. But honesty is a good policy. You'll do fine, you'll sleep well at night and you'll feel good about the example you are setting for your coworkers and the other people who care about you.'"

Integrity often is its own reward, says Hank Paulson (Goldman Sachs). "On a personal level, . . . the only real satisfaction that comes anywhere in the world is from doing good. People like working hard toward some goal, and making progress toward that goal. That is where satisfaction comes from. But the goal has to be for good. No one is happy with himself if he's not a good person."

Jorge Paulo Lemann (Gillette) agrees that not only is integrity a good business practice, but practicing it will help you feel good about yourself. "Your relationship with other people will be much better and in general you'll do much better. It makes the world a better place and I think people are interested in making the world a better place."

Self-respect. It's being able to hold your head up high. It's having the trust of the people for whom you are responsible. The leaders we interviewed would tell you these are the greatest advantages of living with integrity. For those of you who were hoping for something more, they add this promise: You will be successful in the end.

During the past year, we have witnessed integrity in the most unexpected places (and discovered it lacking in some of the places we felt surest to find it). Despite rumors to the contrary, integrity still exists in the highest echelons of corporate America as well as on factory floors and oil rigs, inside fast-food restaurants and in vast cubicle mazes. Perhaps one of the most poignant and powerful examples of personal integrity is one we witnessed recently in a person we always respected, but never as much as he deserved.

Greg Smith is a good and honest man who has made his career in corporate insurance—admittedly a profession that struggles with its reputation. From his home in San Antonio, Texas, Smith recalled an ethical decision that became a defining moment for him and in many ways symbolizes what this book is all about.

He was writing an insurance policy for a new commercial client. As he filled out the paperwork, the client asked him to change the policy's effective date to cover a small claim that had occurred a few days earlier. Fudging the date would save the client hundreds of dollars, but at what expense? Smith's integrity.

"Well," he said quietly and without hesitation, "then when is the next time you want me to lie to *you*?"

Smith had reached his line in the sand. He had planned for this moment long ago, and he knew he would not cross it at any price. Not for anyone.

He won an integrity battle—and a lifelong customer. The client paid $25,000 for his original policy but has since spent nearly $1 million with Smith over the past few years. On top of the original property and casualty insurance, he now buys his business insurance, life insurance and estate planning through Smith. Why? Because he knows he can count on Greg Smith's integrity. He knows his agent has something more valuable than power, prestige or money.

He has the Integrity Advantage.

And soon, we hope, so will you. May you enjoy the journey.

About the Authors

Adrian Gostick is an award-winning business author and lecturer. With coauthor Chester Elton, he wrote the critically acclaimed *Managing with Carrots* and *The 24-Carrot Manager*. Visit their Website at www.carrotbooks.com. He has published articles in dozens of national business magazines and holds a master's degree in strategic communication and leadership from Seton Hall University. He can be reached at agostick@allwest.net

Dana Telford is a researcher and guest lecturer at Harvard University and a management consultant. He has presented his work and advised clients in North and South America, the Middle East and Europe. He earned an MBA from Harvard Business School. He can be reached at danatelford@earthlink.net.

Please visit theintegrityadvantage.com.

To order additional copies of

The
Integrity
Advantage

Telephone 1-800-748-5439

Or visit www.gibbs-smith.com

Discounts are available for orders of more than twenty-five books.

_____ (# of copies) The Integrity Advantage), Gibbs Smith Publisher, P.O. Box 667, Layton, Utah 84041

Bill my : ☐ Visa ☐ MC   Signature _____

☐☐☐☐ ☐☐☐☐ ☐☐☐☐   Expiration: ☐☐ ☐☐

Daytime phone (_____) _____

SHIP TO: Name _____

Address _____

City _____ State _____ Zip _____

Payable in U.S. funds only. Postage and handling: $2.75 for one book, $1.00 for each additional book not to exceed $6.75; International $5.00 for one book, $1.00 for each additional book. We accept Visa, MC, checks ($15.00 fee for returned checks) and money orders. No Cash/COD. Call 1-800-748-5439 or 1-801-544-9800 or mail your order.

Book Total: _____

Applicable sales tax (CA, UT): _____

Postage and handling: _____

TOTAL AMOUNT DUE: _____

Reaction to *The Integrity Advantage*

Without integrity as the cornerstone of your business and personal life, nothing else really matters. This book is a must-read for everyone, but most importantly for businesspeople who believe the only measure of their company's value is in its financial statement.
  —Mike S. West, vice chairman, Rayne Corporation

Finally, a wonderfully crafted book that addresses a fundamental value that every businessperson should have and enhance. Using examples from top business leaders, the authors give 10 characteristics of a person with integrity and a thought-provoking four-step process for self-evaluation and improvement. Reading this book is an imperative for anyone involved in business!
  —Gregory S. Boswell, president,
  National Association for Employee Recognition

If you have ever wondered if integrity is really worth it in business you owe it to yourself to read *The Integrity Advantage* by Gostick and Telford. The authors prove that keeping your word not only lets you sleep well, but in the long run builds profitable businesses. This is a book for every manager and every employee in a time where honesty really is the best policy. It is the best business book I've read in at least a year!
  —Chester Elton, coauthor *The 24-Carrot Manager*

Holding your course in the turbulent waters of today's business environment has never been more tested. The authors of *The Integrity Advantage* give you a pointed road map and temperature check for doing the right thing first, and then doing the right thing even better!
  —Anne C. Ruddy, executive director, WorldatWork

You've addressed a fundamental and critical element in all relationships which, regrettably, has received scant attention in business literature. Your . . . essential contribution will instruct, reinforce, and remind us that the primary objective in building ourselves is achieving integrity and trusworthiness throughout our lives.

—Cathy Quinn, Ph.D., clinical psychologist,
Beverly Hills, California

Leadership inspires us to reach for our most elevated values. *The Integrity Advantage* is, by definition, essential to success as a leader. We enthusiastically endorse and follow those individuals who call forth the striving we all have for personal integrity.

—Dr. Lynn Newman, MBA faculty,
Pepperdine University